Our Lady Untier of Knots

Novena

By

Clinton R. LeFort

January 2016

History of the Devotion

The devotion to Our Lady Untier of <u>Knots</u> was originally started in Germany thru a man named Wolfgang Langenmantel (1568-1637) Because of the hardships he was facing in his own marriage he turned to recourse to a pious and holy Jesuit Confessor and director of the Ingolstadt Monastery. Wolfgang visited the monastery and over the course of several days visited the holy Confessor several times; at the end he finally resolved his marital problems. It had been known that the Holy Jesuit had himself received a visit form the Blessed Virgin Mary which he spoke of as "Mother Thrice Admirable."[1]

It was customary at the time, during wedding ceremonies for the maid of honor to to join

---

[1] See All About Mary at the University of Dayton Institute for Mary.

together the arms of the bride and groom with a piece of ribbon. At the time of one of the last visits to Fr. Rem, Wolfgang gave to Fr. Rem the ribbon which had joined he and his wife. Fr. Rem performed a ritual whereby he lifted up the knot and untied the knot one by one then flattened out the ribbon before Wolfgang and his bride. The ribbon had become completely white again. Wolfgang and his bride were able to keep there marriage intact and avoid divorce.

Many years later the grandson of Wolfgang, a Canon of St. Peter's (1666-1709) whose name was Hieronymou Ambrosious Langenmantel commissioned a work of art to commemorate the new century and it was to honor the memory of the Langenmantel family. The painter Johann Georg Schmittdner was commissioned for the work. Schmittdner took the theme of the original "miracle" recalled of Wolfgang, Sophie and Fr. Rem. Mary was placed in the center of the "miracle" while the dove above Mary referred to Mary being the Spouse of the Holy Spirit. Mary untying the knots represented the grace that Mary obtained for the couple thru Fr. Rem, who untied the knots of our difficulties in our lives. The devotion is international in scope today because of the recent recommendation by Pope Francis who firs encountered the devotion and picture while he was a student in Germany, then brought it to Argentina.

The first reference to the devotion to Mary as untied of knots is recalled by St. Irenaeus, a first century Martyr and Father of the early Church, who is recorded as meeting the Apostle John.

Knots in our Lives?

What are the knots in our lives, which we ask Mary to untie and to resolve according to the Will of God? All of us face difficulties everyday. Some of our difficulties are easily resolved, but often we come encounter difficulties which seem insurmountable or even impossible for us to resolve. These difficulties require extra help from God, so we turn to Mary, who is honored under this particular title, to assists us in our spiritual, material and every kind of struggle. Jesus said whatever you do to the least of my brethren you do to me, so we turn to Mary and honor her, since we know that placing all of our needs before God can only result in a peaceful resolution. Are we pressed with problems in our family, friends, work, finances, finding work or making friends? Have we recently moved to a new place and know no one or are we caught in a rut in our lives where we need new direction? We can always turn to Mary in our needs. St. Bernard said this many centuries ago.

And the Virgin's name was Mary." Let us speak a little about this name, which is said to mean "star of the sea," and which so well befits the Virgin Mother. Rightly is she likened to a star. As a star emits a ray without being dimmed, so the Virgin brought forth her Son without receiving any injury. The ray takes naught from the brightness of the star, nor the Son from His Mother's virginal integrity. This is the noble star risen out of Jacob, whose ray illumines the whole world, whose splendor shines in the heavens, penetrates the abyss, and, traversing the whole earth, gives warmth rather to souls than to bodies, cherishing virtues, withering vices. Mary is that bright and incomparable star, whom we need to see raised above this vast sea, shining by her merits, and giving us light by her example.

Look To Mary

"All of you, who see yourselves amid the tides of the world, tossed by storms and tempests rather than walking on the land, do not turn your eyes away from this shining star, unless you want to be overwhelmed by the hurricane. If temptation storms, or you fall upon the rocks of tribulation, look to the star: Call upon Mary! If you are tossed by the waves of pride or ambition, detraction or envy, look to the star, call upon Mary. If anger or avarice or the desires of the flesh dash against the ship o f your soul, turn your eyes to Mary. If troubled by the enormity of your crimes, ashamed of your guilty conscience, terrified by dread of the judgment, you begin to sink into the gulf of sadness or the abyss of despair, think of Mary. In dangers, in anguish, in doubt, think of Mary, call upon Mary. Let her name be even on your lips, ever in your heart; and the better to obtain the help of her prayers, imitate the example of her life: "Following her, thou strayest not; invoking her, thou despairest not; thinking of her, thou wanderest not; upheld by her, thou fallest not; shielded by her, thou fearest not; guided by her, thou growest not weary; favored by her, thou reachest the goal. And thus dost thou experience in thyself how good is that saying: 'And the Virgin's name was Mary.'" (St. Bernard, Homily II, Missus Est, 17)

Who has not faced difficulties in life? Who has called on Mary, and not received help, says St. Bernard. In other words, according to the Holy Doctor of the Church, Mary can answer all of our needs regarding eternal salvation, if not directly then as mediatrix to Jesus. One word spoken to Mary in prayer is more valuable than a million spoken to someone else who hasn't the power to understand your prayer. As children of God, Mary has a special role in our life and the Holy Spirit tells her what words fail to say The Holy Spirit speaks to Mary's heart, for us.

Day 1

Make the sign of the cross

Say the Act of Contrition. Ask pardon for your sins
and make a firm promise not to commit them again.

Oh my God I am heartily sorry for having offended
you. I detest all my sins because I dread the loss of
Heaven and the pains of Hell. But most of all,
because I offended you, oh my God, who are all
good and deserving of all my love. I firmly resolve,
with the help of your grace, to confess my sins, to
do penance, and to amend my life. Amen

Make the meditation of the day.

Say the decades of the rosary

Finish with the Prayer to Our Lady the Untier of Knots

Meditation for Day 1

Mary, I entrust the difficulties of my life into your hands. As Simeon and Anne praised the child which you held in your arms, so I, too, place these knots found in my life in your hands to be untied and resolved with the grace that can only come from you.

Thank you, Dear Mother.

Mary, Untier of Knots, pray for me.

The one who seeks grace, finds it in Mary's hands.

PRAYER TO MARY, UNTIER OF KNOTS

(Closing Prayer)

Blessed Virgin Mary I come to you today under the title of Our Lady Untier of knots. You know yourself the many difficulties we face in this "valley of tears." Come to my aid in this need …… I place before you and your Son, Jesus Christ, the Word Incarnate and King of the Universe.

Mary, Untier of Knots, I place my trust in You.

Day 2

Make the sign of the cross

Say the Act of Contrition. Ask pardon for your sins and make a firm promise not to commit them again.

Oh my God I am heartily sorry for having offended you. I detest all my sins because I dread the loss of Heaven and the pains of Hell. But most of all, because I offended you, oh my God, who are all good and deserving of all my love. I firmly resolve, with the help of your grace, to confess my sins, to do penance, and to amend my life. Amen

Make the meditation of the day.

Say the decades of the rosary

Finish with the Prayer to Our Lady the Untier of Knots

Meditation for Day 2

Mary, I come to you today with these prayers of petition, so that you can help me at this stage in my life. Ask God to untie the knots I find in my life, especially these… I rely upon you intercession and hope that with your help I can once again live at peace and harmony with God in my life.

Mary, Untier of Knots, pray for me.

Mary offered all the moments of her day to God.

PRAYER TO MARY, UNTIER OF KNOTS

(Closing Prayer)

Blessed Virgin Mary I come to you today under the title of Our Lady Untier of knots. You know yourself the many difficulties we face in this "valley of tears." Come to my aid in this need …… I place before you and your Son, Jesus Christ, the Word Incarnate and King of the Universe.

Mary, Untier of Knots, I place my trust in You.

Mary, Untier of Knots, pray for me

Day 3

Make the sign of the cross

Say the Act of Contrition. Ask pardon for your sins and make a firm promise not to commit them again.

Oh my God I am heartily sorry for having offended you. I detest all my sins because I dread the loss of Heaven and the pains of Hell. But most of all, because I offended you, oh my God, who are all good and deserving of all my love. I firmly resolve, with the help of your grace, to confess my sins, to do penance, and to amend my life. Amen

Make the meditation of the day.

Say the decades of the rosary

Finish with the Prayer to Our Lady the Untier of Knots

Meditation for Day 3

Mary, like the bride and groom at the wedding feast of Cana turned to you in their need. They had no wine for their celebration, so I turn to you, since my life is filled with the knots and complications that the world has brought into my life. The world, the flesh, the devil are my enemies, but to you I turn at this time, especially in these difficult knots.....I extend the arms of my heart to you at this time in the hope that you can untie these knots and make me whole and at peace with you Son, Jesus Christ.

Mary, Untier of Knots, pray for me.

Turn to Mary, you who desire grace.

PRAYER TO MARY, UNTIER OF KNOTS

(Closing Prayer)

Blessed Virgin Mary I come to you today under the title of Our Lady Untier of knots. You know yourself the many difficulties we face in this "valley of tears." Come to my aid in this need …… I place before you and your Son, Jesus Christ, the Word Incarnate and King of the Universe.

Mary, Untier of Knots, I place my trust in You.

Mary, Untier of Knots, pray for me

Day 4

Make the sign of the cross

Say the Act of Contrition. Ask pardon for your sins
and make a firm promise not to commit them again.

Oh my God I am heartily sorry for having offended
you. I detest all my sins because I dread the loss of
Heaven and the pains of Hell. But most of all,
because I offended you, oh my God, who are all
good and deserving of all my love. I firmly resolve,
with the help of your grace, to confess my sins, to
do penance, and to amend my life. Amen

Make the meditation of the day.

Say the decades of the rosary

Finish with the Prayer to Our Lady the Untier of Knots

Meditation for Day 4

Mary, the entire Church looks to you under this title of Our Lady Untier of Knots for we believe in your powerful intercession in our life. I, too, a sinner, lift up my heart filled with the knots caused by living in the modern world. May I offer these knots to you, especially….. I entrust this most precious gift to you like Mary Magdalen offered the aromatic spices and her tears on the feet of Our Lord. Present these knots to Jesus for me and thru the help of the grace you obtain may my prayer bring greater glory and praise to our Eternal Father, his Incarnate Son, Jesus Christ, and the Eternal

Spirit of Love who lives in our hearts.

Mary, Untier of Knots, pray for me.

Mary is the Sun and no one is deprived of her

warmth.

PRAYER TO MARY, UNTIER OF KNOTS

(Closing Prayer)

Blessed Virgin Mary I come to you today under the

title of Our Lady Untier of knots. You know

yourself the many difficulties we face in this "valley

of tears." Come to my aid in this need ...... I place

before you and your Son, Jesus Christ, the Word

Incarnate and King of the Universe.

Mary, Untier of Knots, I place my trust in

You.

Day 5

Make the sign of the cross

Say the Act of Contrition. Ask pardon for your sins
and make a firm promise not to commit them again.

*Oh my God I am heartily sorry for having offended
you. I detest all my sins because I dread the loss of
Heaven and the pains of Hell. But most of all,
because I offended you, oh my God, who are all
good and deserving of all my love. I firmly resolve,
with the help of your grace, to confess my sins, to
do penance, and to amend my life. Amen*

Make the meditation of the day.

Say the decades of the rosary

Finish with the Prayer to Our Lady the Untier of Knots

Meditation for Day 5

Our Lady Untier of Knots humbly I place these knots of my life in your hands, especially these... which I give to you in the silence and humility of my heart. I know and trust in your mercy in my life. If there is anyone who can help me at this time I look to you. St. Bernard once said we should always look to you in our difficulties, so following his example as well as the entire Church, who turns to you daily, I place these petitions in your loving and maternal care. Place them before the feet of your Son at the altar in Heaven and may my Guardian Angel also speak to you on my behalf

as well as the behalf of my family and friends who

are united in your Son, Jesus Christ.

Mary, Untier of Knots, pray for me.

Mary, with God, is powerful.

PRAYER TO MARY, UNTIER OF KNOTS

(Closing Prayer)

Blessed Virgin Mary I come to you today under the

title of Our Lady Untier of knots. You know

yourself the many difficulties we face in this "valley

of tears." Come to my aid in this need ...... I place

before you and your Son, Jesus Christ, the Word

Incarnate and King of the Universe.

Mary, Untier of Knots, I place my trust in You.

Mary, Untier of Knots, pray for me

Day 6

Make the sign of the cross

Say the Act of Contrition. Ask pardon for your sins
and make a firm promise not to commit them again.

Oh my God I am heartily sorry for having offended
you. I detest all my sins because I dread the loss of
Heaven and the pains of Hell. But most of all,
because I offended you, oh my God, who are all
good and deserving of all my love. I firmly resolve,
with the help of your grace, to confess my sins, to
do penance, and to amend my life. Amen

Make the meditation of the day.

Say the decades of the rosary

Finish with the Prayer to Our Lady the Untier of Knots

Meditation for Day 6

Our Lady Untier of Knots I turn to you today as pilgrims in the Church have turned to you for centuries, but today I come to you under your title of Our Lady Untier of knots, since I believe you can help me to reolve these knots and difficulties which I cannot untie on my own. I present these knots to you, especially … Thank you for hearing my prayer. May I always Honor you and make you known in my life.

Mary, Untier of Knots, pray for me.

You are beautiful, Mary, and there is no stain of sin in You.

PRAYER TO MARY, UNTIER OF KNOTS

(Closing Prayer)

Blessed Virgin Mary I come to you today under the title of Our Lady Untier of knots. You know yourself the many difficulties we face in this "valley of tears." Come to my aid in this need …… I place before you and your Son, Jesus Christ, the Word Incarnate and King of the Universe.

Mary, Untier of Knots, I place my trust in You.

Mary, Untier of Knots, pray for me

Day 7

Make the sign of the cross

Say the Act of Contrition. Ask pardon for your sins and make a firm promise not to commit them again.

Oh my God I am heartily sorry for having offended you. I detest all my sins because I dread the loss of Heaven and the pains of Hell. But most of all, because I offended you, oh my God, who are all good and deserving of all my love. I firmly resolve, with the help of your grace, to confess my sins, to do penance, and to amend my life. Amen

Make the meditation of the day.

Say the decades of the rosary

Finish with the Prayer to Our Lady the Untier of Knots

Meditation for Day 7

Mary, Our Lady Untier of Knots, I hate sin and I hate the devil who causes all kinds of harm in our lives. I come to you today to have you listen to these problems which I face. At times I do not see a way out of My situation, but we believe that you can help us to overcome the knots we face in our life. Please accept these knots, especially….and present them to your Son, Jesus Christ, so that I can find a wise and peaceful resolution to my life again.

Mary, Untier of Knots, pray for me.

You are the glory of Jerusalem, the joy of our

people.

PRAYER TO MARY, UNTIER OF KNOTS

(Closing Prayer)

Blessed Virgin Mary I come to you today under the title of Our Lady Untier of knots. You know yourself the many difficulties we face in this "valley of tears." Come to my aid in this need …… I place before you and your Son, Jesus Christ, the Word Incarnate and King of the Universe.

Mary, Untier of Knots, I place my trust in You.

Mary, Untier of Knots, pray for me

Day 8

Make the sign of the cross

Say the Act of Contrition. Ask pardon for your sins
and make a firm promise not to commit them again.

*Oh my God I am heartily sorry for having offended
you. I detest all my sins because I dread the loss of
Heaven and the pains of Hell. But most of all,
because I offended you, oh my God, who are all
good and deserving of all my love. I firmly resolve,
with the help of your grace, to confess my sins, to
do penance, and to amend my life. Amen*

Make the meditation of the day.

Say the decades of the rosary

Finish with the Prayer to Our Lady the Untier of

Knots

Meditation for Day 8

Mary, Our Lady Untier of Knots, when you visited Elizabeth the child in her womb leaped for joy. I also leap for joy knowing that you are near and can help me with unravel the knots in my life. I humbly implore you to look upon these needs, especially … and …. May it be God's Holy Will to please you in my life and to continue to serve you and your Son, Jesus Christ. I thank you for hearing me and obtaining for me these graces so that I can live untied and unhindered by the temptations in this life so that I can join you and your children in Heaven on day.

Mary, Untier of Knots, pray for me.

Let us go, therefore, full of trust, to the throne of grace.

PRAYER TO MARY, UNTIER OF KNOTS
(Closing Prayer)

Blessed Virgin Mary I come to you today under the title of Our Lady Untier of knots. You know yourself the many difficulties we face in this "valley of tears." Come to my aid in this need …… I place before you and your Son, Jesus Christ, the Word Incarnate and King of the Universe.

Mary, Untier of Knots, I place my trust in You.

Mary, Untier of Knots, pray for me

Day 9

Make the sign of the cross

Say the Act of Contrition. Ask pardon for your sins and make a firm promise not to commit them again.

Oh my God I am heartily sorry for having offended you. I detest all my sins because I dread the loss of Heaven and the pains of Hell. But most of all, because I offended you, oh my God, who are all good and deserving of all my love. I firmly resolve, with the help of your grace, to confess my sins, to do penance, and to amend my life. Amen

Make the meditation of the day.

Say the decades of the rosary

Finish with the Prayer to Our Lady the Untier of Knots

Meditation for Day 9

Mary, Our Lady of Untier of Knots, we love you and honor you. We are creatures who are fallible and weak and that is why I humbly come to you with the knots of my life. Can you help me untie these problems, which I cannot unravel alone, especially … and … and …. I have tried everything that I can humanly do to bring resolution to my life in these matters, but I turn to you as my only sure hope and recourse. I turn to you as a member of your Son, believing and hoping you will assist me in these knots. May I always have the grace to follow and horn you and your Son, Jesus Christ and join you in praising and adoring him in eternity.

Mary, Untier of Knots, pray for me.

PRAYER TO MARY, UNTIER OF KNOTS

(Closing Prayer)

Blessed Virgin Mary I come to you today under the title of Our Lady Untier of knots. You know yourself the many difficulties we face in this "valley of tears." Come to my aid in this need …… I place before you and your Son, Jesus Christ, the Word Incarnate and King of the Universe.

Mary, Untier of Knots, I place my trust in You.

Mary, Untier of Knots, pray for me

Made in the USA
Columbia, SC
21 July 2023

20714559R00024